PABLO PICASSO

By Gini Holland

WORLD ALMANAC® LIBRARY

Please visit our web site at: www.worldalmanaclibrary.com
For a free color catalog describing World Almanac® Library's list
of high-quality books and multimedia programs, call 1-800-848-2928 (USA)
or 1-800-387-3178 (Canada). World Almanac® Library's fax: (414) 332-3567.

Library of Congress Cataloging-in-Publication Data

Holland, Gini.
    Pablo Picasso / by Gini Holland.
       p. cm. — (Trailblazers of the modern world)
    Includes bibliographical references and index.
    Summary: Describes the life and career of Pablo Picasso, discussing his great impact on twentieth-century art.
    ISBN 0-8368-5084-X (lib. bdg.)
    ISBN 0-8368-5244-3 (softcover)
    1. Picasso, Pablo, 1881-1973—Juvenile literature. 2. Artists—France—Biography—Juvenile literature.
[1. Picasso, Pablo, 1881-1973. 2. Artists. 3. Painting, French.] I. Title. II. Series.
N6853.P5H649   2003
709'.2—dc21
[B]   2002034308

First published in 2003 by
World Almanac® Library
330 West Olive Street, Suite 100
Milwaukee, WI 53212 USA

Project manager: Jonny Brown
Project editor: Betsy Rasmussen
Design and page production: Scott M. Krall
Photo research: Diane Laska-Swanke
Indexer: Walter Kronenberg

Photo credits: © 2003 Artists Rights Society (ARS), New York/ADAGP, Paris: 21, 26; © 2003 Estate of Pablo
Picasso/Artists Rights Society (ARS), New York: 13, 15, 17, 19, 20, 24, 27 top, 30, 33, 37, 38, 39; © 2003 Succession H.
Matisse, Paris/Artists Rights Society (ARS), New York: 11; © AP/Wide World Photos: 4, 40, 41; © Art Resource, NY:
37; © Bettmann/CORBIS: 6, 28, 29 top, 33, 38; © Hulton Archive: cover, 8, 12, 14, 24, 26, 27 bottom, 29 bottom, 39;
© Hulton-Deutsch Collection/CORBIS: 16, 32; Scott Krall/© Gareth Stevens, Inc., 2003: 9, 10; Digital image © The
Museum of Modern Art/Licensed by SCALA/Art Resource, NY: 17, 21; Pablo Picasso, *Accordionist*, Summer, 1911,
Solomon R. Guggenheim Museum, New York, Gift, Solomon R. Guggenheim, 1937, © Solomon R. Guggenheim
Foundation, New York: 20; Pablo Picasso, *Family of Saltimbanques*, Chester Dale Collection, Photograph © 2002
Board of Trustees, National Gallery of Art, Washington: 15; Pablo Picasso, Spanish, 1881-1973, *The Old Guitarist*,
1903/04, oil on panel, 122.9 x 82.6 cm, Helen Birch Bartlett Memorial Collection, 1926.253, image © The Art Institute
of Chicago: 13; © Scala/Art Resource, NY: 19; © Tate Gallery, London/Art Resource, NY: 30; © John Bigelow Taylor/Art
Resource, NY: 27 top; © Roger Viollet/Getty Images: 11, 22, 23, 34

Printed in the United States of America

1 2 3 4 5 6 7 8 9 07 06 05 04 03

TABLE of CONTENTS

Words that appear in the glossary are printed in **boldface** type the first time they occur in the text.

CHAPTER 1

NEW ART FOR A NEW CENTURY

By 1935, Pablo Picasso had become a major artistic force and was world famous as cofounder of Cubism and modern art.

It's early in the 1900s. Picasso mixes paint directly on his tabletop, working intently by the light of an oil lamp. It is the middle of the night. He dabs dark blue paint onto light blue paint, shading the face of an old man on crutches. The only bright colors in this painting glow from the basket of flowers that the man carries on his back. Picasso's studio, perched on the top floor of the Bateau Lavoir ("Laundry Boat") building, has no electricity and no running water. His empty cot stands beside the window next to a small stove. His only other furniture is a table and two chairs. Tubes of paint and paintbrushes lie scattered across the floor; his paintings are stacked three-deep against the walls. Picasso, soon to become the best-known artist of the twentieth century, paints until dawn and creates another masterpiece, one brush stroke at a time.

A MODERN WORLD REQUIRES MODERN ART

Pablo Ruiz Picasso was an artistic **prodigy**, a child able to paint and draw as well as or better than adults. His father was an artist and art teacher, and he trained Spanish-born Picasso in the **classical** tradition. This meant Picasso could create drawings and paintings with all the **realism** and true-to-life colors of the old masters of Europe. Picasso had great respect for this kind of work. He once remarked, "Drawing is no joke. There is something very serious and mysterious about the fact that one can represent a living human being with line alone and create not only his likeness but, in addition, an image of how he really is. That's the marvel!"

For Picasso, however, this kind of realism was not enough. While still a young man, Picasso chose to go beyond the limits of art as it was in Europe before 1900. He broke with artistic traditions and moved beyond the work of recording real life. He helped create something new, called **modern art**.

Instead of just showing how things looked in reality, Picasso expressed in visual terms how the world was being restructured and how art itself was an object that you could examine and explore. He broke his images into cubes and planes. He rearranged the elements of faces, bodies, and all physical reality to express a broad range of changing feelings and ideas. He used colors as symbols of moods, such as blues for sadness and pinks for romantic visions. Whether he painted, sculpted, made **collages**, or worked with ceramics, he stretched the ways in which these forms expressed his artistic vision.

Even his friends had a difficult time keeping up with his ideas. His secretary and lifelong friend, the poet Jaime Sabertès, wrote about seeing some of Picasso's new work when the two men were still in their early

Photography Challenges Painters

Photography, still in its infancy when Picasso began his career, was able to capture the way things looked. This quality challenged artists to explore art beyond copying reality. Even in its early years, photographers argued that photography was an art form, since it often expressed the feelings and ideas of the photographer. The challenge—and freedom—for artists was clear: They could now move beyond painting people, animals, and scenes that looked real. Painting could become less realistic and more **abstract**.

twenties: "Picasso has spent his life taking leaps, but he always takes them forward. Hence one should not be too shocked by a picture of his which shatters all accepted convention, for before long he will produce others even more radically different and these, by shocking us still more profoundly, will serve . . . to make us appreciate for the first time those we were about to reject."

Traffic was horse-drawn on Montmartre Boulevard in Paris when Picasso first strolled among its crowds as a young man.

Historical Change Influences Picasso

Artists often respond to the world around them when they work. Picasso found himself in a world where technology, religion, politics, and social rules were all changing faster than in previous centuries. Born in 1881, Picasso struck out on his own in 1900. In his ninety-one years, Picasso lived to see technology progress—from the first radio broadcasts to color television and from the horse and buggy to car and air travel. Women got the right to vote and own property, and their clothing changed from floor-length dresses and wool bathing costumes to miniskirts, pants, and bikinis. Picasso also saw, among other events, two world wars, the Russian and the Chinese communist revolutions, and a civil war in his native Spain. It can be argued that Picasso's art expresses, among other things, the dramatic rate of change in the world in which he lived. As his world changed around him, Picasso used his skills to help change the face of art. He extended the accepted ideas of what art could look like, and he broadened art's range of expression. Art no longer had to look like something in nature in order to have meaning. Art could be an object to think about on its own terms.

A CONTRADICTORY PERSONALITY

It took more than talent for Picasso to become the world-famous artist who helped change the face of modern art. It took a powerful personality as well. Picasso remembered that his mother was impressed with her son's intense character. "When I was a child, my mother said to me, 'If you become a soldier you'll be a general. If you become a monk you'll end up as the Pope.' Instead, I became a painter and wound up as Picasso." He made a powerful impression on people. This helped him gain the respect, support, and friendship of many important art dealers, writers, and other artists.

Picasso's outgoing personality helped him find the friends he needed for intellectual challenge and companionship. During the day, he enjoyed an active social life. Yet, a complicated man with many contradictions, he also thrived on solitude for work. He carved out a great deal of time to create without interruption. He often worked late into the night, taking advantage of the time when most of his companions were asleep.

He treasured family life, but, in addition to two marriages, he had many mistresses and more than one child outside of marriage. When asked about love, he explained "I love what belongs to me, yet at the same time I have a strong urge to destroy. It's the same with love."

Perhaps Picasso's greatest contradiction was his ability to be both completely free and absolutely disciplined. He could ignore any rules about **composition** or color, but he made up new ones that he followed strictly, at least for the time that he chose to work within his new limits. While he loved spontaneity and enjoyed the process of creating, he cautioned about freedom: "Freedom is something you have to be very careful about. Whatever you do you find yourself in chains.

The freedom not to do something means that you're absolutely bound to do something else. And there are your chains."

MASTERING—AND BREAKING—THE RULES

One of the most famous and influential artists of his time, Picasso mastered all the rules of painting and sculpture, and then he broke them. In so doing, he helped change the way art is defined, understood, and enjoyed. He expanded our understanding of the concept of truth with his work, saying, "If there was a single truth, you couldn't make a hundred paintings of the same subject." He himself would often take a subject and create a series of works on that single image, exploring its multiple aspects, moods, and meanings as he moved from one canvas to the next.

He cofounded an important art movement, Cubism, with his friend Georges Braque, but he never limited himself to that style alone. For Picasso, what was important was that each piece of his artwork, whatever its style, stand on its own and express something of himself and his vision to the world. "Repeatedly I am asked to explain how my painting evolved. To me there is no past or future in art. If a work of art cannot live always in the present it must not be considered at all." He wanted his work to be ageless, to always have something to say to every generation.

With his vision, he changed the way we see the world. With his energy and passion, he lived his life as an act of discovery and continuous creative output. As a result, when he died at ninety-one years of age in 1973, he left an enormous legacy of artistic work, now housed in museums, private collections, and public places throughout the world.

Georges Braque, photographed in his studio in Paris in 1955, cofounded Cubism with Picasso.

YOUTH AND TALENT

On October 25, 1881, Pablo Ruiz Picasso was born in Málaga, in southern coastal Spain. Young Picasso did not like most school subjects, but he enjoyed studying art under his father's direction at the School of Fine Arts and Crafts of San Telmo. In 1891, when Picasso was ten, his family moved to La Coruña, on Spain's Atlantic seacoast. One day in 1894, Picasso's father asked him to complete one of his drawings. Picasso did such a masterful job that his father handed over his brushes to his son and declared that he would now quit painting, since Picasso, at age thirteen, had surpassed his own father as an artist.

YOUTHFUL PRODIGY

In 1895, the family moved to Barcelona, where Picasso's father had found a teaching position at the School of Fine Arts. Picasso enrolled as a student. The next year, needing space of his own in which to work, Picasso rented his first studio on the Calle de la Plata in Barcelona. He was fourteen years old.

In 1897, his painting *Science and Charity* won an honorable mention at the National Exhibition of Fine Arts in Madrid. He passed his college entrance exams at age fifteen and began his studies in Madrid at the Royal

Academy of San Fernando. But after two years of study, Picasso began to move frequently between Madrid, Barcelona, and Paris as he worked to establish himself as an artist.

IMPORTANT FRIENDSHIPS AND SUPPORT

In 1899, he left Madrid and returned to Barcelona on the Mediterranean Sea. There he met his friend Carlos Casagemas, a painter with whom he shared a studio on the Calle Riera de San Juan. In Barcelona, he also met his lifelong confidant and secretary, Jaime Sabartès, who later helped set up a museum of Picasso's work in Barcelona, the city where the two first met.

Picasso first published his drawings in *Joventud*, a Barcelona review, in 1900 and made his first trip to Paris with Casagemas that year. Although the two friends were planning to go to England, they stayed instead in Paris, falling in love with the city and its artistic community. This was the beginning of Picasso's long and productive connection with France.

On this first trip to Paris, Picasso sold three drawings to an important gallery owner named Berthe Weill, who would later

become the first dealer for the artist Henri Matisse. She bought three paintings of bull-fights from Picasso for 100 francs. Then he so impressed the art dealer Petrus Meñach that he was paid 150 francs a month in exchange for all he could paint. While in Paris, Picasso worked in a studio at 49 Rue Gabrielle, sharing it with Casagemas.

In addition to meeting art dealers and gallery owners, Picasso and his friend enjoyed the city's art museums. The two saw paintings by the innovative artists of their day: Van Gogh, Gauguin, Degas, and Toulousse-Lautrec, as well as those of classical artists, such as Leonardo da Vinci's *Mona Lisa*, which hangs in the Louvre.

MAKING A LIVING

Since young Picasso was making a living—although a poor one—through his art, he thought that he could live independently in Paris. He preferred the life of a hungry artist to that of an art teacher or some other occupation with a regular income. Looking back on this choice, Picasso explained: "When you have something to say, to express, any form of submission becomes unbearable in the long run. You have to have the courage of your vocation and the courage to live by that vocation. The 'second profession' is a trap! I was often penniless myself, but I always resisted any temptation to live by any means other than my painting."

In the meantime, Picasso's friend Casagemas had a love affair that ended badly. Picasso thought that he could help his friend recover by bringing him back to Málaga. The two of them had such long hair and shabby clothes that the local hotels were afraid to risk renting to them—they looked too poor to pay the bill! Picasso turned to his aunt and uncle for help, but they found their nephew's ragged clothes and artistic life objectionable. So after several days, Picasso went on to Madrid. Tragically, Casagemas returned to Paris, where he committed suicide. Picasso grieved for his friend and wished he had been able to help him. For many years, his painting *The Burial of Casagemas* was the first thing one saw on entering his studio.

LA VIE EN BLEU

Picasso returned to Barcelona in September of 1900. He began to travel frequently, moving from Barcelona back to Madrid in February of 1901, then traveling to Paris for the second time at the end of March and then back to Barcelona at the end of December.

It was during this second stay in Paris that Picasso, still mourning the loss of Casagemas, began his Blue Period. During this time, he was living in the cheapest neighborhoods, and he concentrated on the subjects at

In 1900, pedestrians bustled on La Rambla de las Flores in Barcelona, the Spanish city on the Mediterranean Sea to which Picasso often returned.

hand: the poor people of Paris and, on his trips back home, the poor of Barcelona. During his Blue Period, he captured people on canvas in sad or serious moments, washed in blue colors.

Yet despite his unhappy mood, things began to go fairly well for him. He had his first art exhibit. He met people in Paris who helped him, and he formed lasting friendships with many important artists and writers of the day. One of his close friends was Max Jacob, an influential writer and artist, whose use of symbols and dreams had a major impact on the symbolist and **surrealist** schools of art.

When Picasso returned to Paris for a third time, he shared a room on the Boulevard Voltaire with his new friend Max Jacob. Since the room had only one small bed, they took turns: Picasso worked by night and slept by day, while Jacob worked during the day and crawled into the bed after Picasso got up at night. They were so poor that, at one point, Picasso actually burned a number of his drawings in order to keep warm. Art collectors today might pay thousands or even millions of dollars for these works, had they been saved.

As with Casagemas, Picasso's friendship with Max Jacob ended in tragedy. When World War II erupted, Jacob (a former Jew who had converted to Catholicism) died in a Nazi concentration camp. Picasso's life was deeply marked by this and other world events, although some critics insist he lived, through his art, above it all.

During his Blue Period, Picasso painted *The Old Guitarist* over another painting he had made. A woman's face from the old painting still shows through the man's left shoulder, an effect called pentimento. The painting now hangs in the Art Institute of Chicago.

Pablo Picasso, Spanish, 1881-1973, *The Old Guitarist*, 1903/04, oil on panel, 122.9 x 82.6 cm, Helen Birch Bartlett Memorial Collection, 1926.253, image © The Art Institute of Chicago.

CHAPTER 3

BREAKING RULES

While he broke the rules of traditional art and painting, Picasso also broke many of the rules of the middle- and upper-class society into which he was born. In 1904, Picasso's Blue Period gradually came to a close. He moved into the Bateau Lavoir, at 13 Rue Ravignan (now Place Emile-Goudeau), in Montmartre. This artists' neighborhood, on the Right Bank of the Seine, was famous for its wild nightlife at places such as Le Moulin Rouge and the Lapin Agile. Here Picasso began to live a **Bohemian** life in earnest. This meant, among other things, that he worked when he felt like it, did not worry about middle-class social rules, and spent more time worrying about art and ideas than about money and appearances.

The Moulin Rouge (Red Mill) of the Montmartre section of Paris was one of Picasso's favorite haunts. The artist Toulouse-Lautrec created paintings featuring the nightclub's dancers, helping to make the place famous.

LA VIE EN ROSE

Picasso began to socialize with circus performers, harlequins, actors, and artists' models—people rarely accepted as equals by Europeans of the upper classes. He stopped painting life with a sad blue haze and started seeing life through rose-colored glasses. Thus he entered his Rose Period, painting his new friends in warm pinks and rose pastels. He washed his work in these soft fantasy colors while he continued to free himself from the rules of the **bourgeois** society in which he had grown up.

The following year, in 1905, Picasso met the writer and editor Guillaume Apollinaire. Picasso's friend Sabartès once wrote, "The presence of Apollinaire was important because he was cultivated, intelligent and imaginative—three qualities which were essential for the atmosphere surrounding Picasso and which were indispensable elements for the intellectual revolution which was in preparation." In addition, Apollinaire was important because he introduced Picasso to artist Georges Braque.

Shortly after meeting Apollinaire, Picasso met the well-known American writer and art patron Gertrude Stein, who promoted the careers of many celebrated talents living in Europe, including American writers Ernest Hemingway and F. Scott Fitzgerald. Picasso began to sculpt that year. In 1906, Picasso met the famous artist Henri Matisse. He also painted his now well-known *Portrait of Gertrude Stein*. When a friend complained that it didn't look like her, Picasso just laughed and insisted that Stein would look like her painting in time.

Picasso pursued a young model, Fernande Olivier, who also lived in the Bateau Lavoir. When she refused his offers of love, he superstitiously built a small shrine to her in his studio and kept a candle lit on either side of her portrait. In the end, Picasso won her away from

As with most of Picasso's Harlequin paintings, this 1905 *Family of Saltimbanques* was huge—over 7 feet (2 m) square. Rose and red hues dominate, but blue accents and serious faces bring hints of Picasso's Blue Period into this Rose Period work.

her lover, and she began to live with him. He was quite possessive and did not want her to pose for other artists. Always a night owl, he often sketched her while she

Gertrude Stein

When Fernande Olivier was planning to leave Picasso, she wrote to Gertrude Stein. She wanted Stein's help in publishing her memoirs about living with the famous artist. Olivier received no reply. She later found out that Stein was also writing about Picasso in Stein's soon-to-be-famous *Autobiography of Alice B. Toklas*. Here is an excerpt from Stein's work about posing for Picasso:

Then there was the first time of posing. . . . In those days there was even more disorder, more coming and going, . . . more cooking and more interruptions. There was a large broken armchair where Gertrude Stein posed. There was a couch where everybody sat and slept. There was a little kitchen chair upon which Picasso sat to paint, there was a large easel and there were many very large canvases. It was at the height of the end of the Harlequin period when the canvases were enormous, the figures also, and the groups. . . . Fernande was as always, very large, very beautiful and very gracious. She offered to read La Fontaine's stories aloud to amuse Gertrude Stein while Gertrude Stein posed. . . . Picasso sat very tight on his chair and very close to his canvas and on a very small palette which was of a uniform brown grey color, mixed some more brown grey and the painting began. This was the first of some eighty or ninety sittings.

Author Gertrude Stein, pictured here at her desk in 1936, encouraged and promoted many writers and artists, including Picasso.

slept and also painted her in many poses from their daily life. At one point they befriended an orphan girl who had camped in their foyer. He also sketched and painted this new friend. His relationship with Fernande lasted from 1906 until 1912. In this way, Picasso created a temporary family life on his own terms, outside the rules of middle-class society.

In 1906–1907, while still living with Fernande at the Bateau Lavoir, Picasso created hundreds of notebook drawings and paintings in preparation for what was to become a masterpiece. His friends named it *Les Demoiselles d'Avignon*.

Painted in 1907, *Les Demoiselles d'Avignon* was Picasso's massive challenge to the art world. With this work, Cubism was born. The painting now hangs in the Museum of Modern Art in New York City.

In this painting, Picasso combined a number of artistic styles, including African art. It was so wild that many of these same friends hated it or thought he was joking. Apollinaire disliked it; Matisse thought it was a horrible hoax; Gertrude Stein called it "a veritable cataclysm;" Stein's art-collector brother, Leo, simply labeled it "a horrible mess." Even the artist Georges Braque found it unsettling, but he began to understand it better when Picasso went on to paint *The Three Women*. In fact, most art historians now consider *Les Demoiselles d'Avignon* "the birth of Cubism."

CHAPTER 4

CUBISM: AN ARTISTIC REVOLUTION

In 1908, after Picasso painted *Les Demoiselles d'Avignon*, he and fellow artists Braque, Matisse, and André Derain began a revolutionary conversation in both words and paint. The ideas of these artists created a new art movement called Cubism. An art critic provided this name when he described Cubism as art that broke objects into cubes.

Picasso described Cubism this way: "Many people think that Cubism is a kind of transitional art or an experiment that will mature and be capable of producing different results. They are the ones who have not understood Cubism. It is simply an art which is concerned with form—and when a form is created, it exists and lives its own life."

Why Not Try to Understand the Songs of a Bird?

Picasso often claimed that he did not paint to be understood. He painted, as he put it, out of necessity. It was what he was born to do. He said:

Everyone wants to understand art. Why not try to understand the songs of a bird? Why does one love the night, flowers, everything around one, without trying to understand them? But in the case of a painting, people have to understand. If only they would realize above all that an artist works of necessity, that he himself is only a trifling bit of the world, and that no more importance should be attached to him than to plenty of other things which please us in the world, though we can't explain them.

Picasso and Braque challenged each other to paint in new directions. Georges Braque brought **pointillism**, among other things, to Cubism. Pointillism is a technique where small dots or points of color are built up in place of flat brush strokes. The result is a depth and shimmer of color. It was also used in place of lines to create shapes with color alone.

Picasso had already found new ways to break up forms into their essential flat shapes and planes. His revolutionary masterpiece *Les Demoiselles d'Avignon* had set up some of the ideas that the two artists began to explore. They took ideas from one another and pushed them further. For example, they showed an object or person from several sides at the same time. One painting might show a nose and mouth in profile but with the eyes and chin facing forward. Thus images were broken up and rearranged in compositions that forced people to look at familiar subjects from a changed point of view.

In spite of their serious competition, the two artists enjoyed their painted conversations immensely. In fact, in the summer of 1911, Picasso teased his friend by

The face is recognizable but the body dissolves into cubes and triangles in Picasso's 1909 *Portrait of Ambrose Vollard*. The portrait now hangs in the Pushkin Museum of Fine Arts in Moscow.

painting *The Accordionist*, which showcased Braque's favorite instrument and used Braque's painting style, to the astonishment of his friend. Not to be outdone, Braque answered with his own *Man with a Guitar*, Picasso's favorite instrument. Braque used the same figure and chair and the same triangular cubist construction that Picasso had used in *The Accordionist*. These two works are good examples of the way Cubism was born out of artistic challenge and the exchange of visual ideas.

WAR YEARS

Picasso's *Accordionist*, painted to tease his friend Georges Braque, hangs in the Solomon R. Guggenheim Museum in New York City.

It can be said that Picasso painted his way through World War I, the Spanish Civil War, and World War II without ever trading his brush for a gun. In this way, he was spared some of the suffering that many Europeans, including some of his closest friends, had to endure first hand. During World War I (1914–1918) his native Spain was neutral, so Picasso was not drafted to fight for his country. He had to live with the same fears, curfews, and rationed supplies that most other Europeans struggled with, but he was otherwise free to paint, travel, fall in love, and live a fairly normal life.

In 1912, two years before the outbreak of World

Note: "World War II" should read
"World War I" at the top of page 21.

War II, Picasso began dating Marcelle Humbert, whom he called Eva. They moved to the South of France, where Picasso joined Braque and the artist André Derain. Here he began to extend his ideas of his Early Cubism phase, and he developed Synthetic Cubism. With Synthetic Cubism, Picasso added bits and pieces of recognizable forms, such as numbers, corrugated cardboard, and newspaper headlines, to his work. These became the first collages, where paper, wood, **oilcloth**, and other fragments of reality were added to paintings. He pursued this phase of Cubism until 1921. Picasso's Cubism had three main phases, starting with Early Cubism, then moving to Synthetic Cubism, and finally to Crystal Cubism, in which he emphasized squares, sharp lines, and glassy, mineral colors. In all cubist works, composition (the way things are arranged and balanced against each other) is a key aspect. Sometimes, especially in more abstract pieces, composition was the main subject of the work; it was what the painting was "about."

Many people did not like what Picasso and other Cubist artists were doing. In fact, Cubism was so annoying to many that Apollinaire, an editor at the Soirées de Paris, lost his job because he published a

Georges Braque's response to Picasso's *Accordionist* is this *Man with a Guitar*, now displayed in the Museum of Modern Art in New York City.

Apollinaire and the Statue Affair

Apollinaire, born Wilhelm (or Guillaume) Apollinaris de Kostrowitzky, was a colorful figure in French society. He is considered a modernist poet and was a key person in leading the way to surrealism in art and writing. Born to Angelica de Kostrowitzky, a Polish gambler living in Italy, who claimed that Apollinaire's father was the Swiss-Italian aristocrat Francesco Flugi d'Aspermont, Apollinaire changed his name and, as a youth, passed himself off as a Russian prince. Primarily a poet, he was a well-known force in all **avant-garde** movements in turn-of-the-century Paris. His study of Cubist painting, *Peintres Cubistes* (1913), helped make Cubism well known and better understood by the general public.

French writer Guillaume Apollinaire (1880–1918) is pictured here at Yvetot, France, in the summer of 1913.

He was occasionally involved in scandal and was at least once accused of thievery. As a result of a misunderstanding, both Apollinaire and Picasso were accused of stealing **Iberian** statues from the Louvre museum in Paris! In fact, Apollinaire's secretary had received the statues in 1911 and claimed he did not realize that they were stolen goods. In the end, the charges of thievery were dropped. Apollinaire published his poetic impressions of his war experiences a few months before his death of influenza in the great epidemic of 1918.

picture of one of Picasso's cubist sculptures. Some thought Cubism was too "intellectual," while others felt it was not intellectual enough. Some complained that it was too sophisticated to understand, while others argued it was too childish to bother with, insisting, "my child can do that." But Picasso and his fellow Cubists knew how to promote themselves and their ideas. They convinced many art galleries, dealers, and critics that they were creating something new and important. They continued to explore Cubism and gained a strong following in the international art world.

A TIME OF CREATIVITY AND LOVE

Although he did not have to fight in World War I, these war years were not without anxiety and some loss for Picasso. His friends Braque and Apollinaire were drafted when the war broke out in 1914, and his mistress Eva died the following year.

In spite of these sad circumstances, World War I soon became a period of creativity and some delight for Picasso. He met his first wife, the ballerina Olga Koklova, on a trip to Rome in 1916. His friend Jean Cocteau, the famous writer, artist, and filmmaker, invited Picasso to come and design both scenery and costumes for a Russian ballet company production of *Parade*. Koklova was a ballerina in the troupe.

Picasso's first wife Olga (née Koklova) Picasso (1896–1955) and their son Paolo, photographed in France around 1930.

The costumes Picasso designed were pure fantasy. He had some dancers dress as trees while others wore cardboard buildings on their heads. This was too extreme for most audiences, who booed Picasso's work along with the ballet. If this discouraged Picasso, it did not keep him from continuing to design for the ballet and stage in the coming years, in both London and Paris.

Picasso designed costumes and this set for The Ballets Russes performance of *Pulcinella*, directed by Sergei Diaghilev, with music by Igor Stravinsky.

Picasso and Olga honeymooned in Biarritz, where he painted his famous *The Bathers* in 1918. Olga led Picasso to a glittering social life with her ballet and symphony connections. They also enjoyed seaside vacations. Picasso combined his images of dancers, the swimmers he sketched on the beach, and statues he saw in Rome and elsewhere in Italy. He dropped his Cubism style in favor of **neoclassical** painting but kept a certain element of fantasy: the people were thick, larger than life, like statues.

On the surface, Picasso's family life seemed happy. He and his wife Olga had a son, Paolo, born in 1921. But in 1927, when Paolo was about six, Picasso began an affair with a woman named Marie-Thérèse Walter. Some say that of all the women in his life, Picasso loved her the most. Picasso and Walter had a daughter, Maia, in 1935. When Olga found out about Maia, she left Picasso, taking Paolo with her. Although Picasso lived with other women after this, he did not marry again until 1961, when, at the age of eighty, he married Jacqueline Roque.

BETWEEN THE WARS

Picasso, now an acknowledged master painter, was still a willing student. In 1928, he learned to weld from Julio Gonzalez, a Spaniard living in France. Welding allowed Picasso to make metal sculptures and to fuse all kinds of "found objects" together. For example, celebrating his

Picasso the Pack Rat

In the words of his friend Jean Cocteau:

Picasso kept everything he was given: bottles of eau de Cologne, bars of chocolate, loaves of bread, packets of cigarettes and boxes of matches, and even his old shoes, which were lined up under a table. . . . He had never thrown anything away, even hoarding useless household utensils, the old oil-lamp which lit the canvases of the Blue Period, a broken coffee-grinder . . . he considered that anything that had come into his hands formed part of himself, contained a portion of himself, and that parting from it was equivalent to cutting off a pound of flesh.

Photographer and artist Dora Maar, Picasso's dedicated companion and mistress, posing here beside one of her own paintings.

love of bullfights, Picasso joined a bicycle seat and handlebars together to make a bull's face and horns. As a kind of artistic recycler, Picasso picked through junkyards for his materials. Now his studio was not only piled with paintings and drawings, but also with junk that might find its way into his welded sculptures.

In early 1936, Picasso, living in France, met Dora Maar, an accomplished photographer and aspiring painter, and he began a seven-year romance with her. He drew and painted her in numerous styles, from Cubist to surrealist. She worked alongside Picasso, learning from him, photographing him at work, modeling for him, and painting, among other things, her own versions of his portraits of her.

It was Maar who suggested that Picasso move to the attic studio of 7 rue des Grands Augustins, a seventeenth-century mansion in Paris that was the site of a well-known story by Honoré de Balzac. Balzac's story was about an artist who struggled to create a masterpiece. Picasso liked the idea of becoming Balzac's fictional artist. In fact, Picasso created one of his finest masterpieces in this attic studio.

THE GUERNICA MASTERPIECE

In July 1936, civil war broke out in Picasso's native Spain. A **pacifist**, Picasso hated war. He refused to fight, even though he did not want the military dictator, General Francisco Franco, to win. Instead, he painted his famous *Guernica*, an antiwar protest on canvas.

The Spanish town of Guernica was horribly bombed on April 27, 1937. Picasso's massive painting, which he created during May and June of that year, shows the suffering of the innocent people who were hit. Displayed at the Spanish Pavilion of the 1937 World Exhibition in Paris, this painting gave Picasso worldwide recognition.

Dora Maar photographed his progress on the painting and is even reported to have added a few brushstrokes herself. Art historians have studied these photographs for decades. From them, scholars have found seven clear stages through which the painting *Guernica* traveled during its creation. For many, the journey that Picasso made on this canvas is considered as important as the finished masterpiece. Picasso himself once said, "I've reached the moment when the movement of my thought interests me more than the thought itself." This movement is well recorded in Dora Maar's photographic portrait of Picasso at work.

Picasso's immense 1937 antiwar masterpiece *Guernica* now hangs in the Museo National Centro de Arte Reina Sofia, Madrid.

The Eiffel Tower, shown here at an earlier exhibition, dominated the 1937 World Exhibition's skyline, where Picasso's *Guernica* was displayed.

Spanish Civil War

In 1936, General Francisco Franco led a military fight against the middle class liberals, socialists, and leftist factions of the Second Republic that had replaced the Spanish monarchy in 1931. Franco promoted fascism, which dictates government control—often brutally exercised—over all aspects of daily life, including politics, art, literature, and people's actions and words. Fascism began in Italy with the rise of the dictator Benito Mussolini.

Many young liberal Europeans from France, England, and elsewhere volunteered to fight in this civil war against Franco. They saw the Spanish Civil War as an important freedom cause for which many gave their lives. Supporting conservatives and traditional landowners, Franco succeeded in winning his civil war at a tremendous cost and with help from Nazi Germany and fascist Italy. More lives were lost and more property was destroyed in the Spanish Civil War than in any other war in Spain's history. Franco imposed fascism and ruled Spain as a self-appointed regent and military dictator from 1939 through 1968. He died in 1975.

Spanish dictator General Francisco Franco, leader of fascist troops during the Spanish Civil War, gave this fascist salute on September 6, 1939.

One of the bombed streets of Guernica. The Basques laid responsibility for this brutal attack on German volunteers in the Spanish Civil War.

In July 1936, male and female militia fighters marched proudly together at the beginning of the Spanish Civil War.

Dora Maar: More Than a *Weeping Woman*

Born Henriette Théodora Markovitch in Russia on November 22, 1907, Dora Maar was an established and talented surrealist photographer by the time she met Picasso in 1937. An intellectual with her own career, she combined striking physical beauty with a voice that many have described as unique, beautiful, and even extraordinary. Dora herself credits her voice with winning Picasso's love. "She was anything you wanted," Picasso once told James Lord, "a dog, a mouse, a bird, an idea, a thunderstorm. That's a great advantage when falling in love."

She was the subject of Picasso's *Weeping Woman* series. Not only did she make an important photographic record of his painting process, but she also posed for the woman raising a lamp in the middle of his *Guernica* painting. When Picasso abandoned her for another woman, she was extremely upset and lived her remaining thirty years in religious contemplation and seclusion. When she died in 1997, a number of original works by Picasso were found among her belongings and auctioned off for considerable sums of money. In fact, she had many mementos from him, including little sketches on rocks and matchbooks. In spite of living in Picasso's shadow, her own work remains important. Some of her photographs, such as *Portrait of Ubu*, *Silence*, and *29 rue d'Astorg*, are well-known emblems of the Surrealist movement.

One of the many crying woman paintings for which Picasso's mistress Dora Maar posed, *The Weeping Woman* now hangs in the Tate Gallery in London, England.

Some have criticized Picasso for not fighting in any wars, saying he removed himself from the suffering. Others complained that he was too intellectual about the conflicts. But Picasso cared about politics. He often took a strong political stand in both his antiwar paintings and his personal actions. For example, in a conversation with Jaime Sabartès, the photographer Brassaï (born Gyula Halász) once asked if Picasso would return to Spain for the opening of the Picasso Museum in Barcelona. This museum would house Sarbartè's collection plus, according to Sabartès, "everything Picasso has offered the city of Barcelona since 1917."

Sabartès explained Picasso's position, answering, "He'd certainly like to. He would love to see Barcelona again. But as you well know, in 1939, the day the Treaty of Burgos was signed, he swore he would never set foot in Spain again as long as the Franco regime lasted. So, despite his desire, he is resisting." In the end, this meant that Picasso never set foot in his native country after the Spanish Civil War of 1936–39, even though he lived another thirty-plus years.

Too old to fight in World War II, Picasso endured the hardships of Nazi-occupied France along with the French. He was forbidden to exhibit his work while the Nazis occupied Paris. Yet, while the French **Vichy** government—which collaborated with the Nazis—ruled daily life, Picasso's artistic life remained free. In art he could express his desire for liberty and his hatred of Nazism and fascism. In a comment of Picasso's published in 1945, at the end of World War II, we see how Picasso viewed his art as an instrument of battle: "No, painting is not done to decorate apartments. It is an instrument of war for attack and defense against the enemy."

During World War II, Picasso divided his time
between Paris and the south of France. In Paris he lived
at 7 Rue Augustins. Here his daily routine began when
his maid, Ines, brought him coffee with milk and two bis-
cuits. He had breakfast in his large copper bed
covered with a white-spotted cowhide blanket. His maid
lit the wood-burning heater in the middle of the room.
As the room warmed, he received friends. By afternoon,
he was ready to work but was often interrupted by visi-
tors. His evenings were his own: he painted well into the
night, enjoying his quiet solitude.

CREATIVITY AND COMMUNISM

Just after World War II, Picasso began working at Madame Ramiéa's pottery shop in Vallauris, near Cannes in the south of France. Picasso lived near Vallauris for ten years. It was at Madame Ramiéa's that he decorated ceramics and worked with clay, taking the local potters' basic shapes and adding to them. With his fame, he put this country town—once well known for its ceramics—back on the map. The townspeople were grateful enough to celebrate his birthday with a festival. They once held a bullfight in his honor as well. In 1948, he exhibited many of his decorated pots and plates at La Maison de la Penseé Française in Paris. He continued his work in ceramics throughout the rest of his life.

Picasso worked on this vase in Madame Ramié's pottery workshop on the French Riviera.

ALWAYS LEARNING

In 1947, Picasso began to make **lithographs**, which are prints made from drawings produced on limestone using grease pencils or oiled brushes, among other things. These drawings must be done in reverse and require a great deal of technical skill to print. Up to five hundred prints can be made from a single stone. Picasso continued to make lithographs until the end of his life, when he was in his nineties. In 1950, at age seventy-seven, he learned to make **linocut** prints, cutting his drawings into linoleum blocks. He made over three hundred linocut blocks in the next four years, often using this method to make posters for his own ceramics exhibitions.

Love and Loss

In 1943, Picasso met Françoise Gilot. They lived together starting in 1946, mostly in the South of France. They had a son, Claude, in 1947 and a daughter, Paloma, in 1949. But Françoise left Picasso at the close of 1953. Picasso once admitted that he treated women either as goddesses or doormats. In either case, he often failed to treat women as his equal. He had treated Dora Maar as both a goddess and then, at the end of their relationship, as a doormat. Picasso left Maar for Françoise, but then he suffered and mourned when Françoise left him.

Picasso's partner Françoise Gilot is shown here with the couple's daughter, Paloma, in 1952.

Having survived the Second World War, Picasso felt that the communist ideals of social equality and shared wealth would help humanity live in peace. Therefore, he joined the French Communist Party in October 1944. In 1948, after the war, he flew to Communist-occupied Poland to participate in the Russian Communists' first Peace Congress. The Communist Party was happy to have this famous artist in their camp. One French Communist "cell," as local groups called themselves, even took his name as part of their own: Cellule Interentreprise du Parti Communiste Français Pablo Picasso.

The Party demanded much time and support from Picasso, especially in the form of posters for their rallies. In fact, at one point their demands were so great that Picasso commented that if he had joined the Communist Party earlier, "I would not have been able to become Picasso." He simply would not have found the time. Also, it is unlikely that he would have been allowed to explore art in his own way. The Communist Party had very narrow ideas about what art should look like. In fact, the Communist Party preferred something they called Socialist Realism, which showed realistic—but ideal—scenes of socialist heroes. These were usually more like illustrations and propaganda than fine art, and Picasso certainly knew the difference. He often struggled to find ways to both please himself and please the Communist Party.

For communism, Picasso was willing to make something different if his first offerings were not accepted. He was not, however, willing to bow to the artistic rules of Social Realism. For example, Picasso created a variety of his famous peace doves for Party posters, but the Party often sent them back, suggesting he rework them. Given his standing in the art world, this was an astonishing insult. But Picasso did not take it as such. Instead, he humbly accepted the Party's requests for changes and usually managed to make something that the Party felt it could use. Working at the request of Communist Party officials, he frequently made posters and other works that satisfied his own artistic ideas and the party's needs at the same time. He was pleased to receive both the 1951 Stalin Peace Prize and the 1962 Lenin Prize for his contributions.

AN ARTISTIC ICON

By the 1950s, Picasso was world famous and extremely popular. He himself became a kind of icon as his name and face became synonymous with modern art. His fame came not only because of his ability as an artist but also because of his ability to promote himself. He had learned to advertise himself and to take advantage of his connections in the art world in order to promote his fame. Aside from this self-promotion, the most important reason for his fame was his ability to produce so much art. He was extremely productive, always making something new.

Although he never visited the United States, he was very popular there. His U.S. popularity reached its highest point in the 1940s, before his communist sympathies became too well known. Many Americans, on learning of his communist beliefs, liked him less. Some conservative members of the U.S. Congress even spoke out against him during the 1950s, when anti-communist feeling ran high, and called his art dangerous. In spite of this, in 1957, the Museum of Modern Art in New York joined the Art Institute of Chicago in sponsoring a huge exhibit of Picasso's art in honor of his seventy-fifth birthday. This retrospective looked back on the artist's work throughout his life.

The Art Institute of Chicago now displays a number of important "Picassos" in its galleries, including *The Old Guitarist*, 1903, from his Blue Period. The city of Chicago is also home to an immense Picasso sculpture, a 50-foot-tall (15-meter) metal creation on permanent display outside the Chicago Civic Center. Museums throughout the world, especially in Russia, Spain, and France, prize their Picasso collections.

Picasso designed this imaginative sculpture for the Civic Center in Chicago, Illinois, and had it built to his specifications.

"Life Is Not Logical"

As evidence of abuses of power in the Soviet Union and elsewhere increased, many criticized Picasso's choice to remain a loyal Communist. Publicly, he insisted, "Family matters are not discussed in public." But as these abuses became known, Picasso privately worried, "while they asked you to do ever more for the happiness of men . . . they hung this one and tortured that one. And those were innocents. Will this change?"

Picasso's old friend Jean Cocteau called Picasso's decision to join the Communist Party his first antirevolutionary gesture. How could Picasso, who revolutionized art by bending all its rules, join a political organization that dictated such blind obedience? Picasso agreed that this was not logical but simply shrugged and said, "life is not a very logical business." He was loyal to the Party for the rest of his life, although he tried, from 1953 on, to retire from politics and spend most of his energy on his art.

CHAPTER 7

PICASSO'S LASTING IMPACT

As an older man, Picasso turned the jump rope for his young children Claude and Paloma. He made cardboard wings so that his son could jump higher. The wings would rise and fall gracefully from the boy's shoulders as he skipped over the rope. Then Picasso would turn back to his canvas to paint another dove.

ANOTHER LEGACY: PICASSO'S CHILDREN

In terms of age, Picasso in the 1950s was an old man in his seventies. But in terms of his energy and productivity, he was still at the height of his power. In fact, when he married his second wife, Jacqueline Roque, in 1961, he was eighty, and he still painted daily. Jacqueline

Picasso enjoyed a warm relationship with his son Claude, photographed here on August 21, 1955.

became his favorite model. In 1963, he painted 150 portraits of her. She was quiet, peaceful, but intensely interested in Picasso's work. In this way, she kept him company and often spent much of her day watching him work. She was impressed with his ability to make art from scraps that others might ignore, saying, "You can't leave even a bit of thread lying about without him making something from it."

Although the two did not have any children together, Jacqueline ran Picasso's household and helped him care for his children when they visited on holidays. In all, he had four children: his son Paolo with his first wife Olga, his daughter Maia with his mistress Marie-Thérèse Walter, and Claude and Paloma with his mistress Françoise Gilot.

In general, Picasso made little separation between his life with people and his life with art. He gave both people and art his creativity, humor, passion, and full emotional connection. His generosity for causes was legendary. He gave both money and artwork to many relief agencies, as well as to political, artistic, and social causes. He also gave money and art to friends in need and strangers who wrote to him, including Spanish refugees for whom he paid for transportation, clothing, debts, and food. He once sent a picture of a dove to a young boy who wrote to him that his mother would like one.

In 1955, Picasso's daughter Maia posed with two of her father's sculptures.

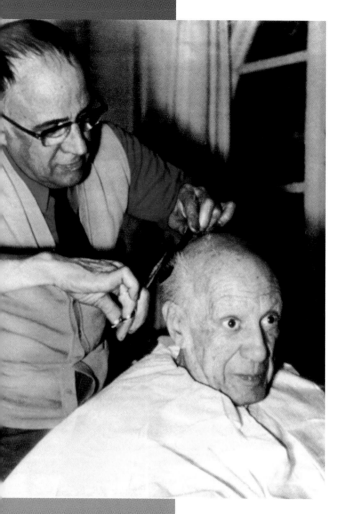

Eugenio Arias cut Picasso's hair for twenty-six years but would not take money, so Picasso always paid him in art.

ALWAYS PRODUCING

In his seventies and eighties, Picasso worked with paper and cardboard, cutting out designs that he used as patterns for metal sculptures and for impressions that would be sandblasted into concrete. His Chicago metal sculpture is one well-known example of this work.

He lived in a number of places in the south of France during his last decades: Antibes, Vallauris, Cannes, Vauvenargues, and Mougins. From 1963 until his death, Picasso worked in his studio at home in the hills above Cannes. He loved animals, from his pet dachshund Lump to his two snails, which he gently fed every day.

He died on April 8, 1973, at ninety-one years of age, at Mougins. The following December, one of his early paintings, *Seated Woman*, sold to an American collector for the record price of $800,000. The monetary value of his work has been increasing ever since.

AN ARTIST FOR ALL TIME

Picasso took art in directions it had never traveled before. For the building blocks of his own work, he took freely from traditional European painting styles, classical sculpture, African art, and other innovative artists of his own day. As a master of his craft, he used the entire known art world, past and present, to create his own artistic expressions. "When there is anything to steal, I steal," he proudly declared. He meant that he used the artistic ideas of all artists to speak in his own terms. The work of artists who had come before him and the work of his admired contemporaries gave him a vast artistic vocabulary with which to express himself. With that vocabulary, Picasso created a tremendous body of work full of variety. He made a great impact on the world of art both in his own time and for future generations.

A man of peace, Picasso energetically celebrated both art and life throughout his long artistic career.

Picasso's Periods

Blue Period, 1901–1904
Rose Period, 1904–1906
Cubist Period, 1908–1915

The first of at least ten major periods, Picasso's Blue Period focused on paintings of the poor of Paris and Barcelona. His Blue Period is one of his best known. His more cheerful Rose Period followed the Blue Period. In his Cubist Period, he broke his subject matter into cubes and planes, among other things. Other distinct periods of his work, some of which overlap, include these:

Neoclassical Period, 1917–1924

During this time, Picasso created drawings inspired by the classic painter Ingrès. He designed fanciful sets and costumes for the ballet *Parade*. His paintings during this period are inspired by Greek and Roman sculpture of the museums and streets of Rome and by the myths and classical art of the past, as well as the dancers and beach-bathers he saw while living in Italy.

Barbaric Period, 1925–1929

Picasso filled his work with monsters and skeletons during this period, and he aggressively deformed and rebuilt the shapes of women. In this time between two world wars, he explored his darker thoughts about the world in general.

Boisgeloup Period, 1930–1935

Marie-Thérèse Walter modeled for him while he lived in Boisgeloup. He sculpted in a variety of media, carving wood and making plaster casts, reliefs, and works of iron.

Wartime Period, 1935–1945

During the Spanish Civil War, Picasso's lover, Dora Maar, inspired a series called *Weeping Woman*, expressing the tragedy of war. This series led to Picasso's famous antiwar painting, *Guernica*. Maar herself was an accomplished artistic photographer and painter, and she may have added some brush strokes to this masterpiece.

Vallauris Period, 1947–1954

Picasso began working with ceramics while he lived outside of Vallauris in the South of France. Here he also made sculptures from recycled objects.

Dialogue with the Old Masters Period, 1955–1962

Picasso painted his response to works by Manet, Poussin, Valázquez, Delacroix, and other master painters of the past. This created a kind of visual conversation between himself and these artists.

Last Works, 1962–1973

In 1963, Picasso created fifty paintings about himself as an artist, with the theme "painter and his model." In 1968, his *Erotic Series* resulted in 347 drawings on sexual themes. In 1971, Picasso offered 156 etchings with more erotic subjects. At age ninety-two, in 1972, he produced his final self-portrait.

Picasso also created numerous works in other styles, including his "one liners," such as his harlequin group done in 1918, in which he draws entire figures in one line, never allowing his pencil to leave the paper.

TIMELINE

1881	Pablo Picasso is born on October 25 in Málaga, Spain
1900	Travels to Paris for the first time
1901	His Blue Period begins
1904	Moves to Paris and rents Montmartre studio
1904	His Rose Period begins
1906-1907	Paints *Les Demoiselles d'Avignon*, with its African influence, which creates the beginning of Cubism
1908	Begins working with Georges Braque and together they create Cubism
1915	Designs ballet scenes and costumes in Rome; meets his first wife, Olga Koklova
1921	His first child, Paolo, is born
1928	Learns to weld and begins making metal sculptures
1935	His daughter Maia is born
1906	Civil war breaks out in Spain; Picasso meets Dora Maar
1907	Paints the antiwar painting *Guernica*
1944	Joins the Communist Party in October
1947	His son Claude is born
1949	His daughter Paloma is born
1905	Awarded the Stalin Peace Prize
1957	The Museum of Modern Art in New York and the Chicago Art Institute celebrate Picasso's seventy-fifth birthday with a retrospective of his work
1962	Awarded the Lenin Prize for his contributions to communism through his art
1973	Dies at 91 years of age on April 8

abstract: a type of art that does not show an exact representation of an object, but instead interprets attitudes and emotions using shape, color, design, and composition

avant-garde: a group that creates new directions in the arts

Bohemian: someone with artistic or literary interests who ignores conventional standards of behavior

bourgeois: a group or individual with characteristics concerned with conventions, respectability, and financial safety

classical: in art, a true or realistic representation of the person or object being painted

collages: compositions made by gluing various materials onto a surface

composition: way in which the parts of an artistic creation are arranged and balanced

Iberian: belonging to people of Spain or Portugal

linocut: a print made from a linoleum block into which a picture or design has been cut

lithographs: prints made from pressing onto paper a stone (or, more recently, a sheet of copper or aluminum) that has been treated so that the printing ink sticks only to the drawn areas

modern art: art that has been created since the late 1800s that uses approaches other than classical realism

neoclassical: a revival of classical forms of art

oilcloth: a cloth treated with oil and used as a table covering

pacifist: a person who is strongly opposed to war

pointillism: art that uses clusters of small dots in place of larger brush strokes

prodigy: someone who has extraordinary talent or abilities

realism: giving a visually accurate picture

surrealist: in art, containing elements of reality, combined with fantastic and dreamlike qualities

Vichy: after World War II, an area of France that was governed by the French but in cooperation with Nazi forces

TO FIND OUT MORE

BOOKS

Anholt, Laurence. *Picasso and the Girl with the Ponytail: A Story about Pablo Picasso.* New York: Barrons Juveniles, 1998.

Antoine, Veronique. *Picasso: A Day in His Studio.* New York: Chelsea House Publishers, 1994.

Galassi, Susan Grace. *Picasso's One-liners.* New York: Artisan, a division of Workman Publishing Company, Inc., 1997.

Leal, Brigitte. *Ultimate Picasso.* New York: Harry N. Abrams, 2000.

Meadows, Mathew. *Pablo Picasso.* New York: Sterling Publishing Co., Inc., 1996.

Venezia, Mike. *Picasso.* Danbury, Conn: Children's Press, 1994.

Wakabayashi, H. Clark, ed. *Picasso: In His Words.* New York/San Francisco: Welcome Enterprises, 2002.

INTERNET SITES

The Artchive
http://www.artchive.com/artchive/P/picasso.html
Access images of Picasso's work and information about his evolution as an artist.

Pablo Picasso
http://www.theatreonthesquare.com/picasso/piclink.html
For a brief biography and an extensive directory to articles, prints, posters, and photos.

Chicago, Illinois
http://www.bluffton.edu/~sullivanm/picasso/picasso.html
For color photos of the fifty-foot-high "Chicago Picasso" sculpture unveiled on August 15, 1967.

Picasso—The Early Years, 1892–1906
http://www.boston.com/mfa/picasso/timeline.htm
For detailed timeline of Picasso's life, his inspiration, and online examples of his work.

Spanish Civil War
history.acusd.edu/gen/WW2Timeline/Prelude07.html
For an illustrated chronological outline of key events of the Spanish Civil War and information on Picasso's painting of *Guernica* and the bombing that inspired it.

INDEX

INDEX *(continued)*

About the Author

Gini Holland received her bachelor's degree from the University of Wisconsin-Milwaukee after studying at UW-Madison and the University of Cape Town in South Africa, where she was actively involved in anti-apartheid activities. A teacher of students with emotional behavioral disabilities for seventeen years, she currently provides workshops and produces educational videos for teachers through Milwaukee Public Schools, Office of Staff Development and Instructional Services. She has written over twenty books for young people (including *Mandela* for the Trailblazer series), lives in the Washington Heights neighborhood of Milwaukee with her husband Daniel and three charming cats, and is a devoted fan of her son Noah Tabakin's music and three bands: Tabakin, All Fours, and Little Blue Crunchy Things.